Shall We Dance?

MODERN DANCE

by Wendy Hinote Lanier

FOCUS
READERS

www.focusreaders.com

Focus Readers is distributed by North Star Editions:
sales@northstareditions.com | 888-417-0195

Produced for Focus Readers by Red Line Editorial.

Photographs ©: elvistudio/Shutterstock Images, cover, 1, 14–15, 20–21, 26; Ayakovlev/Shutterstock Images, 4–5, 29; master1305/iStockphoto, 7, 25; Igor Bulgarin/Shutterstock Images, 8; LNP/Rex Features/AP Images, 10–11; Ayakovlev/iStockphoto, 13; futureGalore/Shutterstock Images, 17; elkor/iStockphoto, 18, 22–23

ISBN
978-1-63517-277-5 (hardcover)
978-1-63517-342-0 (paperback)
978-1-63517-472-4 (ebook pdf)
978-1-63517-407-6 (hosted ebook)

Library of Congress Control Number: 2017935140

Printed in the United States of America
Mankato, MN
June, 2017

About the Author

Wendy Hinote Lanier is a native Texan and former elementary teacher who writes and speaks for children and adults on a variety of topics. She is the author of more than 20 books for children and young people. Some of her favorite people are dogs.

TABLE OF CONTENTS

CHAPTER 1

WHAT IS MODERN DANCE?

The show is starting. But what will you see? You never know with modern dance. The style is unpredictable. It blends dance forms. But you will see **emotion**.

Modern dance expresses emotion through movement.

That is because all modern dance expresses human emotion.

Modern dance began in the early 1900s. It was meant to be different from ballet. Classical ballet is very **structured**. Modern dance is not. Early modern dance leaders stressed free movement. Personal

DANCE TIP

Don't plan your movements. Instead, listen to the music. Let your movements take you wherever the music leads.

 Modern dance uses movements from other dancing styles, such as ballet.

experiences were important, too.

Dancers used their bodies as

instruments. Their bodies showed

emotions such as joy or fear.

 Modern dancers perform at a show in Ukraine.

Many movements were close to the floor. In some moves, dancers were almost **horizontal**. Dances often included falling.

Modern dance is still growing. Some ballet movements are still used. But today's **choreography** shows other forms. Dancers also bring their own styles. This is changing the way we define modern dance.

CHAPTER 2

DRESS TO MOVE

Modern dance clothes are not fancy. You just need to be able to move in them. Dancers usually practice in tights without feet. Women also sometimes wear **leotards**. Men wear T-shirts.

Modern dancers can dress however they feel.

Performance clothes are simple, too. Dancers aim to express emotion. Clothes should help do this.

Clothes do not draw attention. The audience should focus on the movements. Women often wear thin, flowing dresses.

DANCE TIP

You might feel uncomfortable while dancing. Take a deep breath and stay focused.

 Bare feet allow you to feel the floor.

Their arms and legs are bare. Men usually wear tights and a shirt.

Most modern dancers perform barefoot. But some wear shoes. They sometimes choose leather or canvas ballet slippers.

CHAPTER 3

BASIC MOVES

Modern dance blends many dancing styles. But there are still some common techniques. Some of them are very old. They started with the first modern dancers.

Modern dancers move freely and naturally.

One is the Graham technique. It is named after Martha Graham. The move is based on **contraction** and release. The contraction happens in your stomach. First, exhale while tightening your stomach muscles. This creates an inward curve to the body. Next, release your stomach

DANCE TIP

Modern dance pushes your body to its limits. Warm up by stretching. It helps you avoid injury.

 Modern dancers practice their techniques in a studio.

muscles when you inhale. Then

lengthen your stomach. Finally,

return to an upright position.

The Humphrey technique is also

old. Doris Humphrey created it.

 Modern dance can be theatrical when dancers show their emotions.

She had a belief. She thought all movement was somewhere between balance and falling. Her technique shows this. It is based on the body's reaction to falling. In this technique, dancers push the limits of their balance. They do a controlled fall. But they recover their balance.

DANCE TIP

Don't be afraid to copy movements from other dancers. Do you see a movement that looks good? Try it for yourself.

EXPRESS YOURSELF

Think of an idea or event that creates a strong feeling in you. The feeling might be anger or joy. It might be sadness or fear. Or it might be some other emotion. Now try to express that feeling to others with only your movements.

There are no set patterns in modern dance. You can express yourself in any way you like. You can use music. But you don't have to.

Modern dance is all about expressing emotions.

ON WITH THE SHOW!

Modern dancers communicate through movement. This movement must be seen to be understood. That's why modern dance is often performed for an audience.

Modern dancers follow the routines created by choreographers.

Many top dancers work with **companies**. Some **specialize** in modern dance. These dancers are well trained. They have practiced all the major dance styles. And they perform wherever there is space. Sometimes it's in a theater. But it could be anywhere, such as a park.

DANCE TIP

Try to keep your weight balanced on the balls of your feet. This allows you to move quickly and smoothly.

 In some performances, modern dancers work together.

There are other ways to see a modern dance performance. You might watch one on television. Or you can find videos online.

 Professional dance companies showcase the best of modern dancing.

The best dancers are picked for a company. But all dancers must start with the basics. Your body must be

trained. It must also be **disciplined**.
Use warm-up exercises. Use
dance techniques. Use movement
patterns, too. After years of study,
you can **audition** for a company.
Who knows? You may turn out to be
a modern dance star!

DANCE TIP

Try doing stretching exercises each morning. Do them before class. Do them in the evening, too. This will improve your flexibility.

FOCUS ON
MODERN DANCE

Write your answers on a separate piece of paper.

1. Write a sentence that describes the main ideas from Chapter 4.

2. Do you think modern dance qualifies as "real" dance? Why or why not?

3. What is the goal of modern dance?
   - **A.** to create an easier kind of dance
   - **B.** to produce a less expensive type of dance
   - **C.** to express human emotion

4. Why don't modern dancers usually wear elaborate costumes?
   - **A.** They don't have enough money.
   - **B.** They don't want to limit their movement.
   - **C.** They think most costumes are ugly.

5. What does **techniques** mean in this book?
   *Modern dance blends many dancing styles. But there are still some common **techniques**.*
       A. movements
       B. types of music
       C. stage sets

6. What does **communicate** mean in this book?
   *Modern dancers **communicate** through movement. This movement must be seen to be understood.*
       A. entertain the audience
       B. share thoughts and feelings
       C. keep the audience guessing

Answer key on page 32.

GLOSSARY

audition
To give a short performance as a test.

choreography
The arrangement of steps and movements for a dance.

companies
Groups of professional dancers.

contraction
The tensing of a muscle.

disciplined
Able to make oneself do the right thing.

emotion
A state of feeling.

horizontal
Flat or parallel to the ground.

leotards
Formfitting one-piece clothes usually worn by dancers.

specialize
To be involved in or participate in a particular type of activity.

structured
Made up of certain types of steps and movements.

TO LEARN MORE

BOOKS

Fuhrer, Margaret. *American Dance: The Complete Illustrated History*. Minneapolis: Voyageur Press, 2014.

Legg, Joshua. *Introduction to Modern Dance Techniques*. Hightstown, NJ: Princeton Book Co., 2011.

Tieck, Sarah. *Dancing*. Minneapolis: Abdo Publishing, 2013.

NOTE TO EDUCATORS

Visit **www.focusreaders.com** to find lesson plans, activities, links, and other resources related to this title.

INDEX